adulteress

adulteress,
a poetry pamphlet by Chloe Hanks

Querencia Press – Chicago IL

QUERENCIA PRESS

© Copyright 2023
Chloe Hanks

ISBN 978 1 959118 44 2

www.querenciapress.com

First Published in 2023

Querencia Press, LLC
Chicago IL

Printed & Bound in the United States of America

for Manu

"I had not asked for such a blood sisterhood; they must love me"
  —Sylvia Plath, Blackberrying

Adulteress

Bodies

                          are shaped

                                                          like trees

           are shaped

                          in winter—

          frozen and

                                        splayed as

                                                                  though limbs

          live a life

of their own.

You took mine

and you distorted

each inch

of my frame

until I snapped—

I am now

something else.

And I

reject it—

1. Solitude can make one thirst for blackberries. Idleness wraps his fingers around your throat and chokes you. Obstructed, the sound of your gargling saliva and choked out breathing could wake the insects from their slumbers. We are all scavengers. We are sifting through lovers like we are foraging blackberries—fingers juiced and bloody with the bite of a thorn.

2. He snouted me from an array of discarded berries, dangling from a vine. Wincing from the bite of a bramble, he sweetened me with words laced with honey. I was, for a while, bitter and sharp, but how easily I would succumb to a natural sweetener. I was rooted and then plucked. A citrus infused cocktail shoved into my grasp, drinking in the scenery, neglecting the cautious ghost of my memories—trust is futile if it is evergreen.

3. The rim of my cocktail glass is sticky with sugar and my fingertips are sticky with the blood of a blackberry. I am without fear and without caution and that is what makes this memory a ghost. He rushed me—frosted limbs aching with cold, we discarded my half full glass as though we might return for it. I wonder if it was still there, clouded by the glow of the morning, unfinished.

4. There was nothing illicit in his pursuit of me, and nothing grand in his gestures; a firework packaged and sold as a slow-burn and I was yet to know. I try to remember the taste of it, but the sticky sweetness has dissipated from memory like sugar dissolving on the tongue; but I remember the weight. He positioned me with blackberries resting on my tongue and began to work the vines and brambles away. It is fascinating, the way bodies and limbs behave like the twines of a tree. He unwrapped the thorns from me so delicately, so his fingers were free from bleeding. He examined me and said, *how has no one snapped you up yet?* I could have answered him—but I silenced him instead.

5. Some blackberries are perfectly sweet—they settle gently on a tongue until the mouth positions itself to squeeze the supple flesh to bursting. Others might be bitter; the sour blackberries can catch you off guard. You are ready and poised for delight and yet you cannot disguise the look on your face as the unthinkable explodes inside your mouth and burns all of the way down.

6. I felt sick with my fill of blackberries.

7. He returned me to my doorstep, bundled in morning frost. A cold hug and no mention of blackberries. I wondered about other fruits for breakfast but the thought of the syrupy taste of blackberries lingered and I was not hungry anymore. I knew in the way he said goodbye without saying my name, I would never see him again.

8. The days that passed began to bleed from the edges and blurred into a week—I thought of him less and wondered less about blackberries. I stopped thinking of how he was hardly responding to me, my phone screen no longer sticky with my juice-smudged fingerprints. My mind no longer occupied by his routine foraging.

9. I started to make smoothies.

10. I developed a taste for other winter berries, there are places you can go to swipe through the options.

11.   The weeks that passed began to bleed from the edges and blurred into a month—I questioned his lack of attentiveness and in response he took the blackberries for himself. I turned to cherries, but they were out of season. I purchased supermarket strawberries that spoiled after a day. I pretended I disliked the familiar taste of a blackberry, but this was a lie.

12.   I took to foraging alone. There is strength in the solitude that would once fill you with voracity. In turn, you are emboldened, bracing your limbs to the elements to plough through the brambles. At one with the bite of a chilling December—

13.   He returned, his indiscretions staining his fingers like blackberry juice. I could taste the lies on his lips but could not define them. It was as though the berries were intoxicating and I was yet to clear my mind of them.

There

is little

beyond

the

entanglement

of limbs.

A little

space for

breathing,

not much

else.

I am twisted

such that

oxygen is

intoxicating.

You ease

pressure

and fill my

lungs

with the juice

of berries.

1. I am looking for my body—

2. Shall we talk about infidelity? Apparently, such is a concept which may creep up on you, twist itself through the brambles to pinch hungry fingertips. I spit him out along with the taste of a cocktail, still a ghost on my lips.

3. I protect my exposed skin from the bruise, my limbs discarded to the wind—

4. I want no part of it.

5. Should I tell her?

6. The words took their time and jumbled somewhat, as though splayed across a vine that has intertwined so many times it is no longer a sentence. I breathed each one in and shaped it on my tongue, expelled them over, and over, until I could recite a confession in a way that would be concise. I told her of the pleasantries and the mistaken identities and the deceitful distortion of limbs.

7. She held herself with the grace of an apple tree—

8. I just wanted a taste.

9. She had questions—each one like the stone of a fruit hitting pale skin from a distance, bruising me like juice. I would reveal new parts of me for her to paint, to try to make it all make sense. The stained memory of his torso wrapped up in my legs, echoing through the silence between us.

10. Who could look upon a girl so stained, trembling with the toxins of fermenting fruits, hear her recounts of claiming the brambles for her own and choose to hear her strength? *A woman.*

11. She would come to me at night. I would roll from the edges of sleep like a creature emerging from the trees—I would offer my truths and she would blanket my skin but neither of us could locate my limbs. She shared her tricks and her politics as a warning for next season. Wisdom like an offering of which I was not yet worthy.

    I was not looking for sisterhood—

12. We are the same, she and I. Beneath the juice stains and bruises, we are one and the same and she knows it. I am beginning to know it. Our bones bare traces of shared fingertips and our saliva bears traces of his. In this, we are united. It is un-natural and yet somehow the most natural of happenstances that might occur in the clutches of vine and bramble. This shared taste for berries.

13. I continue the search for my body and let her go. I look for it in a shape that now feels unfamiliar. I search for it in the bodies of past lovers, revisit our encounters as though I might find a clue. I am looking for my limbs, perhaps I threw them to the wind with my caution. Perhaps I lost them somewhere amongst the fruit trees. Perhaps he kept them to use against me later, like the blackberries.

The same way he kept her from me.

I am

        woman

                  I am

    not wife

                         I am

           girl

                              daughter

              friend

    not wife—

                    I am

                         young

I am

successful

even talented

but not

wife

I am

adulteress

I am adulteress

and somehow

none of the rest

matters.

1. No.

2. Adulteress | Noun
   a woman who commits adultery.

3. What about the blackberries? All I wanted was blackberries, it is not my fault he didn't tell me—

4. "In ancient British folklore, it was believed that blackberries should not be picked after Old Michaelmas Day..." *It is not my fault he didn't tell me—*

5. Do you still taste the blackberries?

6. *It is not my fault—*

7. They are sometimes sharp, bitter.

8. *he didn't tell me he was—*

9. They say the devil landed himself in a bramble bush.

10. *he never said he was* married.

11. *adulteress*

12. We cannot consent to what defines us.

13. All I wanted was the blackberries.

I reject it—

I was

not looking

for sisterhood,

they must love

me.

I

reject it

who could love

me?

a woman

I wash the

blackberries

I am

                                                                    re-acquainted

          with my body

                                          I reject it—

I am

                                                                              not

adulteress—

I am

                                                  clean.

I am

sister

I am

daughter

I am

woman.

ALSO BY CHLOE HANKS

Swift Happenings

I Call Upon the Witches

May We All Be Artefacts

www.ingramcontent.com/pod-product-compliance
Lightning Source LLC
Chambersburg PA
CBHW081346120626
46546CB00011B/3462